THE EDICTS
OF ASOKA

THE EDICTS
OF ASOKA

Edited and Translated by

N. A. NIKAM

and

RICHARD McKEON

THE UNIVERSITY OF CHICAGO PRESS

CHICAGO & LONDON

The University of Chicago Press, Chicago 60637
The University of Chicago Press, Ltd., London

© 1959 by The University of Chicago
All rights reserved. Published 1959
Midway Reprint 1978
Printed in the United States of America

ISBN: 0-226-58611-1
LCN: 59-5748

FOREWORD

Knowledge is power, as Francis Bacon observed more than three hundred years ago; and communication has become, with the subsequent progress of science, an instrument both of power and of knowledge. The numerous paradoxes of our times may be epitomized in the contradiction between the vast increase in means of communication made available by science and technology and the construction of barriers to prevent political intercourse, economic exchange, or cultural influence. Communication is essential to science as a form of inquiry and to democracy as a form of political and social community. Progress in science has provided materials and methods to solve men's problems; it has also made possible the construction of instruments of mass destruction and has been made subject to a variety of political restrictions on inquiry and communication, determined by the variety of political institutions under which they are imposed. Progress in democracy has justified the hope that men have found the means to govern themselves and to promote individual freedom and human rights together with the common good. The power of the instruments of mass communication, which is employed or manipulated differently in different political and social circumstances, has operated to reduce the diversity and the tolerance essential to free communication.

The problems of civilization and society are largely problems of power, and in particular of political and economic power. Yet peace and welfare cannot be secured by political negotiations and economic arrangements alone. When truth and the values of the spirit are treated only as instruments of power, they are transformed by oppositions of power into fanaticism which seeks to impose one view of truth by the use of arbitrary power. The fanaticisms of our times have many causes. One, which is frequently alleged, is the fear, real or trumped up, of an opposed irrational fanaticism. Opposition to fanaticism tends to breed fanaticisms dedicated to the destruction of error. Tolerance seems a weakness in a conflict of powers; yet tolerance is the only rational alternative to organized irrational clashes. The cause of fanaticism, underlying fears and tensions, is ignorance of other historical traditions of thought and culture. Since the close of the First World War men have been shut up, in varying degrees of isolation, within their particular national and cultural traditions. Political thought in particular has often been based during that period on philosophies which have had no place for divergence in thought and, therefore, no respect for the thought of others. They have glorified power and violence, developed the conception that man is controlled wholly by economic necessities, and reduced all other views of values to ideologies by which men may be manipulated and deceived.

Profound as their influence has been, the pursuit of political power and the accumulation of economic goods have not been the unique or even the dominant themes of the history of civilization. Empires have been conquered and have fallen to pieces; classes and peoples have acquired dominance over other men and have been dislodged. Even these movements have been more than clashes of bare power, and they have been influenced by other contemporaneous processes of growth and decay, which they in turn have influenced—religions have spread and declined; cultures have found broad humanistic and spiritual expression and have been turned to selfish and materialistic objectives; reason has been respected for its efficacy in discovering truths and in putting them to work and has been suspected as an instrument of self-deception in rationalizations and of manipulation in ideologies. Epic and tragic poets have depicted clashes of loyalties in which power and position come into conflict with other values and often yield to them. Prophets and theologians have found in charity and holiness motivations for turning from worldly to eternal values. Moralists have appealed to criteria that transcend wealth, fame, and pleasure, and to motives that go beyond selfish interest. Political philosophers have sought in reason and order the foundation for institutions and policy. In addition to revolutions to seize power, men in all cultures have withdrawn from the world in more profound revolutions to set up religious, intellectual, and social communities in which other values would eliminate motivations to power and to acquire material gain. Men secure in power have paused to consider the uses to which power might be put for human betterment.

The Edicts of Aśoka, which are presented in a new edition in this volume, are an outstanding instance of this interaction of power with other values in practical action. They are the proclamations of a man who had acquired enormous power but who had undergone a change of heart. They illustrate the universality of the transformation of power by other values, cultural, social, and moral. They have a universality which transcends national and cultural limits: they seek mutual understanding and confidence based on understanding, and they express ideas which recall the reflections of other thoughtful potentates, like Marcus Aurelius, oppressed by the inhumanity of the operations of power. They have a universality that transcends class limits: they treat mankind as a family in which rich and poor, powerful and humble, have comparable duties and identical rewards. They have a universality which transcends legal and disciplinary limits: they combine the instrumentalities of power with those of education and meditation, and they transform law by love, reason, and tolerance.

Aśoka was an emperor and conqueror who was afflicted by repentance after the short and sanguinary Kaliṅga war. He revealed himself a philosopher in the consequences he draws from his repentance—a political philosopher who expressed himself in proclamations and laws, bounding his country with Rock Edicts to publish his ideals and aims to his neighbors and to his subjects along the frontiers, erecting Pillar Edicts in the important places of his empire to express his moral and social objectives, and dedicating in the Cave Edicts places for religious observance; and a moral philosopher who found a substitute for conquests by arms in conquest by Dharma, by righteousness and morality. He was a religious leader who turned from external observances to internal meditations, from temporal possessions to eternal truths. But above all he was a teacher and, in particular, a teacher of understanding and tolerance.

Aśoka sums up his teaching in a single word, "Dharma." His Edicts make it clear that he conceived his mission to consist in defining, publishing, and propagating Dharma; and the strength and originality of his teaching are underlined by the meaning he gave to that ambiguous term. "Dharma" means the insights and precepts of religion and piety; it also means the principles and prescriptions of ethics and morality. The basic problems of religion and morality are illustrated vividly in the differences among the interpretations that have been made of his teachings:

it is sometimes held that Aśoka's conception of Dharma is essentially Hindu, with a Buddhist tinge; sometimes that it is basically Buddhist, in reaction to Brahmanic ideas; sometimes that it is a generalization of morality, freed from sectarian limitations and that, consequently, both translations of Dharma—the "laws of piety" and the "laws of morality"—have been held to be misleading. This is a controversy which belies the basic teachings of the Edicts. With remarkable clarity, Aśoka recognized the interplay of the various dimensions of the moral life: it reflects a man's duties as determined by his station in life; it reflects a basic order in the universe and a truth discerned in that order; it is a bond uniting people in their associations in families, communities, religions, and nations; it is a fundamental insight, differently expressed in different cultures and religions, which serves as a basis for mutual understanding and peace; it is a guide to action and to self-realization and happiness; it is achieved by action, advanced by instruction, and protected by sanctions, and in turn it provides a basis for policy, education, and justice; it is discovered by self-scrutiny, meditation, and conversion, and it entails renunciation of whatever is inconsistent with it.

The Hindu conception of Dharma concentrated on a rule of life, adapted to the caste and station of each man, by which his whole duty—moral, social, and religious—was determined. Each caste had its own Dharma, but Dharma was also the moral order and the truth, *ṛta* or *satya*, transcending the gods and preserved by them. The Buddhist conception of Dharma turned from the theological and metaphysical aspects of Dharma, as absolute truth and highest reality, to concentrate on its operation in the laws of nature and the relations of men. Dharma is the King of Kings, and it is manifested in the properties, ground, and cause of a thing or a person. Aśoka's conception of Dharma separates it from caste distinctions, religious ceremonials, and theological dogmas; his instruction in Dharma denudes it also of the anagogic interpretations of the career of man developed in Buddhist doctrines of rebirth, the four truths about sorrow, and the ways of deliverance in Nirvana. His Dharma depends on insight and change of heart; it has its applications in individual actions and in human relations; it finds its objective in happiness in this world and in heaven.

Aśoka attributes his own interest in Dharma to repentance for the violence and cruelty of the Kaliṅga war. The change of heart brought about by his reflections on war inspired him to the promulgation of his Edicts by providing an insight for moral reform. His interest throughout is practical in its orientation. He devoted himself to study of Dharma, to action according to Dharma, and to inculcation of Dharma, but the three are inseparable—the study of Dharma translates Dharma into concrete action; action ac-

cording to Dharma provides examples to guide inculcation; inculcation of Dharma, although it depends on instruction, supervision, administration, and
institutions, is achieved finally only by meditation
and study.

The study of Dharma is a study of attitudes and
motives which transforms the customary principles
of action. The change of heart brought about by
Aśoka's reflections on war provided him with the
insight which he employed in all his moral reforms.
The moral equivalent for war is found when the
impulse to conquest by violence yields to the desire
for conquest by morality (*Dharma-vijaya*). Evil actions and good actions are both transformed in the
process. Liberality, thus, is a virtue, but all other gifts
are unimportant when compared to the gift of
morality (*Dharma-dāna*). The gift of morality, in
turn, suggests a basis for the distribution of riches
based in morality (*Dharma-saṁvibhāga*), for acquaintance with men based in morality (*Dharma-saṁstava*),
and for kinship among men based in morality
(*Dharma-saṁbandha*). Sacraments, in like fashion,
have their place in religion, but the sacrament of
Dharma (*Dharma-maṅgala*) makes all other rites and
ceremonials unimportant. Pleasure is a legitimate
motive to action, but true pleasure is pleasure in
morality (*Dharma-rati*), and Aśoka took pleasure in
abandoning the customary royal pleasure tours for
moral tours (*Dharma-yātrās*). The foundation of law

and the guidance of its administration must be found in morality, and therefore Aśoka transformed his system of administration by instituting a new category of high officials charged with the promulgation and supervision of morality (*Dharma-mahāmātras*). Their function was to lead people to attachment to morality and to action according to it as well as to increase the morality (*Dharma-vṛddhi*) of people already devoted to morality (*Dharma-yukta*). People devoted to morality (*Dharma-yukta*) include those inclined to morality (*Dharma-niśrita*), those established in morality (*Dharma-adhiṣṭhita*), and those duly devoted to charity (*dānasaṁyukta*). As one reads the Edicts, the linguistic mark of Aśoka's study of morality becomes apparent in the combination of the word "Dharma" with another word signifying an activity or an attitude which defines Dharma as applied to act or motive and which is itself transformed in that definition. Aśoka's statement of the three dimensions of his purpose uses the same device to express his devotion to study of Dharma (*Dharma-pālana*), to action according to Dharma (*Dharma-karma*), and to inculcation of Dharma (*Dharma-anuśiṣṭi*).

The study of Dharma is not only the basis of concrete action according to Dharma; it is also an action. It is action affecting the principles of action. Study of Dharma achieves the purification of one's fundamental beliefs by returning one's scrutiny to oneself, to self-examination which is the basis of moral action, and to self-exertion which is the means of moral progress. Such knowledge of self leads to recognition of the diversity of ways by which others come to their interpretations of Dharma, and that recognition gives tolerance and the sanctity of life the force of principles. Respect for others is both a consequence and a source of purification of one's own aspirations and beliefs. The conquest of Dharma provides insight into true glory. The gift of Dharma gives meaning to material possessions and material gifts in the light of the kinship of mankind. Devotion to Dharma gives direction to all law and furnishes means to relate physical welfare to happiness. Granted insight and devotion to morality, Dharma can be defined in concrete terms appropriate to the actions of a man and the relations among men. Dharma, in the individual, consists of few sins and many good deeds, of avoidance of evil and passions—of anger, cruelty, rage, pride, and envy—and of cultivation of kindness, liberality, truthfulness, inner and outer purity, gentleness, saintliness, moderation in spending money and acquiring possessions, self-control, compassion, gratitude, and devotion. These are all manifestations of attachment to morality and love of it. Dharma, in human relations, takes the form of a moral code which is repeated in several of the Edicts: obedience to mother, father, elders, teachers, and those in authority; respect for teachers; proper treatment for members of the priestly and ascetic orders, relatives, slaves and servants, the poor and unfortunate, friends, acquaintances, and neighbors; liberality to ascetics, friends, companions, relatives, and the aged; abstention from slaughter of living creatures.

The study of morality and action according to morality take their concrete form for Aśoka himself in the inculcation of morality. There are only two means of inculcating morality—prescriptions and meditation—and prescriptions are ineffective without insight into oneself and the consequences of one's action, without the turning about in one's basic motivations which gives meaning to remorse and conversion, and without meditation on oneself which is the foundation of understanding and purpose. Aśoka's inculcation of morality is a sensitive and shrewd combination of inspiration and constraint, of ideal example and administrative sanction. He instituted officers of morality, charged with instruction, with the imposition of penalties, and with the distribution of honors and gifts; and he included in the duties of other officials the supervision of morality. Several of the Edicts take the form of instructions to his officials in which he tells them, in pragmatic language, that he expects what he conceives to be good to be translated into action and to be put into effect by appropriate measures. He proclaims his adherence to Buddhism, but he draws up his own list of Buddhist texts which treat of morality and instructs monks and nuns to study them. He proclaims tolerance for all faiths, regards all men as his children, and seeks understanding with other countries, near and far, based on confidence and morality. He makes provision for the health and well-being of his people, introduces judicial reforms, provides amenities for the performance of religious observances. He proclaims his readiness to pardon offenses against himself, but he specifies that he has power of retribution if the ways of the offenders are not improved or the offense is unpardonable; he proclaims prescriptions, policies, and penalties; he recognizes the importance of insight, and he is confident that his example will be more effective than his power and will transcend the limitations of time and the confines of his empire.

The Edicts of Aśoka form part of a large body of literature, drawn from all cultures, which seeks power not in domination of men or accumulation of possessions but in conquest of self, in understanding of others, and in contemplation of truths within the scope of reason and goods within the scope of action. It finds expression sometimes in art and poetry; sometimes in religious meditation, philosophical reflection, or humanistic or scientific inquiry; sometimes in the labors by which the mechanisms and materials required for human welfare are developed and controlled. It sometimes erects a city of God, a republic of letters, a commonwealth of mankind, or an academy of science removed from the rivalries and vices of the city of men. It sometimes lays down precepts to guide the sage or the saint, the humble man or the sinner, and to make him immune to changes of fortune and threats of power. It sometimes provides insights and motivations by which human communities are transformed and human beings are liberated for the realization of potentialities unsuspected and inaccessible in other societies.

The classics of this literature may take on a new importance and a new power in the world today. They may recall us to the ideal of tolerance of divergent opinions and open up the way to build communities which take their strength from diversity and freedom and which recognize the possibilities of a world community based on a like tolerance and diversity and guided by a sense of the responsibilities imposed by the present world situation. The progress of communication has made unavoidable world community of some kind; insight into the values of tolerance, reason, love, and sensitivity derived from the reflections of poets, saints, philosophers, and statesmen will provide means by which to make it a genuine community based on genuine communication. Such insight will provide no weapons for the struggle for power which is also a consequence of progress of communication; but struggles for power are seldom won by either opponent—they are often forgotten together with their protagonists, or recorded as a memorial to what was destroyed. Their causes are removed by peace and order and understanding.

RICHARD McKEON

PREFACE

The purpose of this edition of the Edicts of Aśoka is twofold: to make the Edicts available in simple idiomatic English and to present their teachings in intelligible sequence. Many translations of the Edicts are available. For the most part, however, translators have been inhibited—by a desire to remain faithful to texts which are often fragmentary, to reproduce the language and form of expression of the original, and to reflect the atmosphere and attitudes of the times—from expressing the high ideals and straightforward methods of Aśoka in a language suited to his thoughts. The present translation seeks to give the Edicts a modern expression, but without distortion or anachronism; it avoids inversions and archaisms; it makes explicit the conjectural meanings and hypothetical connections which are present even in more literal and cautious versions.

The customary arrangement of the Edicts is according to archeological kind and geographical location—Rock Edicts, Pillar Edicts, Cave Edicts. They have been arranged in this edition to permit them to tell a sequential story: I: Aśoka's description of the edicts and their relations to each other and to their circumstances. II: His account of his experience in the Kaliṅga war which led him to the policy put into effect in the Edicts. III: His purpose in promulgating Dharma or morality. IV: The means he used in carry-

Preface

ing out this policy. V: His interpretation of Dharma. VI: The applications of Dharma, universal and particular.

This arrangement is intended to provide the reader with means by which to come to his own interpretation of the Edicts and their significance rather than to impose a system on them or to read a doctrine into them. The Edicts should speak for themselves. Each Edict is translated in its entirety. Four of the longer Edicts—Pillar Edict VII, Rock Edicts V and X, and the Maskī Rock Edict—have been broken into parts to fit the arrangement, but for the most part the Edicts have been printed as single units, even when their contents go beyond the limits of the sections in which they are placed. Clear indications are given in the text and Table of Contents of the location and relations of the parts of the four edicts which have been divided. The effect of the reordering of the Edicts should be to make it easier to understand them as Edicts—the operation, objectives, and assumptions —rather than to translate them into a moral code, a philosophic system, or religious credo. Further information concerning the Edicts is found in the Introduction; speculation concerning Aśoka's conception of Dharma is found in the Foreword.

Aśoka's Edicts are relevant to the world today. Aśoka faced a problem of tensions and fears among social classes, religious sects, peoples, and nations; he sought a constructive policy to avoid war by advancing human welfare and happiness. He sought to establish the community of all mankind on moral law, on Dharma, rather than on conquest; he sought to purify religious observances and to eliminate doctrinal disputes and sectarian intolerance by identifying the common moral ideal underlying divergent interpretations of Dharma; he sought to elevate moral practice, not by prescriptions and imperatives (which he thought of little value) but by meditation and insight (by which he sought to translate the whole of morality, politics, and religion into two interdependent obligations—to respect others and to perform good deeds). Aśoka thought of his problem in a remarkably broad geographic scope—embracing not only the whole of India but extending three thousand miles beyond its boundaries. The problem today is the problem of mankind, of a commonwealth of men, of a world community; it is, as Aśoka recognized his problem to be, a moral problem of clarifying the common aspirations on which community can be established and of making pluralism of beliefs concerning that common end a source of enrichment and unification rather than a cause of restriction and dissension.

We are grateful to our colleagues in the International Institute of Philosophy: Professors Raymond Klibansky (McGill University, Montreal, Canada), A. J. Ayer (University College, London, England), and Julius Ebbinghaus (Marburg, Germany) and Dr. A. C. Ewing (Cambridge, England) for reading and criticizing the translation.

We have consulted the following texts, and the reader is referred to them for a variety of versions of the Edicts and commentaries on them:

B. M. Barua, *Asoka and His Inscriptions* (Calcutta: New Age Publishers, 1946).

Jules Bloch, *Les Inscriptions d'Asoka* (Paris: "Les Belles Lettres," 1950).

E. Hultzsch, *Inscriptions of Asoka, Corpus Inscriptionum Indicarum*, Vol. I (Oxford: Clarendon Press, 1925).

Radhakumud Mookerji, *Asoka* (London: Macmillan & Co., 1928).

G. Srinivasa Murti and A. N. Krishna Aiyangar, *The Edicts of Asoka (Priyadarśin)* (2d ed.; Madras: Adyar Library, 1951).

Ramavatara Śarma, *Piyadasi Inscriptions* (Patna, 1917).

W. Schumacher, *Die Edikte des Kaisers Asoka* (1948).

Amulyachandra Sen, *Asoka's Edicts* (Calcutta: Indian Publicity Society, 1956).

D. C. Sircar, *Inscriptions of Asoka* (Delhi: Government of Indian Publications Divison, 1957).

Vincent A. Smith, *Asoka: The Buddhist Emperor of India* (3d ed.; Oxford: Clarendon Press, 1920).

A. C. Woolner, *Asoka Text and Glossary*, Vols. I–II (Oxford: Oxford University Press, 1924).

In consultation with Dr. A. N. Upadhye, M.A., D.Litt., Professor of Sanskrit and Prākrit, Rajaram College, Kolhapur, we have gone through the original text and made our own version, taking into account existing translations. Shri K. V. Raghavacher, M.A., Assistant Professor of Philology, Maharaja's

College, Mysore, has been very helpful in preparing the text. Professor George V. Bobrinskoy and Dr. Hans von Buitenen, of the University of Chicago, made many suggestions and criticisms from which we have profited.

This edition of the Edicts of Aśoka forms part of the collection of texts planned by the International Institute of Philosophy under the title "Philosophy and World Community." The collection is to consist of a small number of texts which are to be translated and published in as many languages as possible. The collection is planned by an Editorial Committee composed of G. Calogero (Rome), J. Ebbinghaus (Marburg-Lahn), R. Klibansky (Montreal), Chairman, J. Lameere (Brussels), and R. McKeon (Chicago). The first volume in the series was a German translation of John Locke's *A Letter concerning Toleration*. This English translation of the Edicts of Aśoka is the second volume.

The International Institute of Philosophy was assisted in the preparation of the manuscript and the publication of *The Edicts of Aśoka* by a subvention secured through the good offices of the International Federation of Philosophical Societies from the International Council for Philosophy and Humanistic Studies.

N. A. NIKAM
RICHARD McKEON

MYSORE UNIVERSITY
and
UNIVERSITY OF CHICAGO

CONTENTS

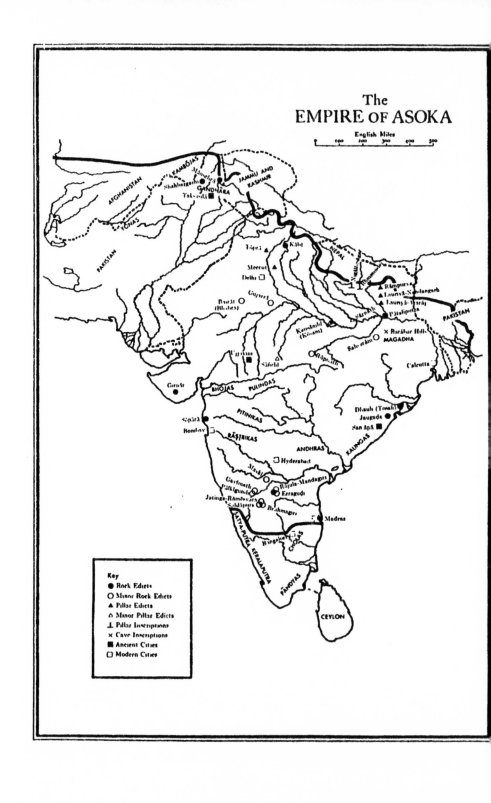

The
EMPIRE OF ASOKA

English Miles

AFGHANISTAN

KAMBOJAS

YONAS

PAKISTAN

Mansehra
Shahbazgarhi
GANDHARA
Taksasila

JAMMU AND
KASHMIR

NEPAL

Tugra
Kalsi
Meerut
Delhi

Bairat
(Bhabra)

Gujarra

Rampurva
Lauriya-Nandangarh
Lauriya-Araraj
Sarnath
Pataliputra

PAKISTAN

Kausambi
(Kosam)

Sahasram
MAGADHA

× Barabar Hills

Calcutta

Ujjain
Sanchi

Rupnath

Girnar

BHOJAS
PULINDAS

PITINIKAS

RASTRIKAS

Sopara
Bombay

Dhauli (Tosali)
Jaugada

San Api

KALINGAS

ANDHRAS

Hyderabad

Maski

Gavimath
Palkigundu
Jatinga-Ramesvara
Siddapura
Brahmagiri

Rajula-Mandagiri

Erragudi

Madras

SATIYAPUTRA KERALAPUTRA

Hingakut

CHOLAS

PANDYAS

CEYLON

Key
● Rock Edicts
○ Minor Rock Edicts
▲ Pillar Edicts
△ Minor Pillar Edicts
⊥ Pillar Inscriptions
× Cave Inscriptions
■ Ancient Cities
□ Modern Cities

INTRODUCTION

Aśoka, one of the greatest of the Indian emperors (*ca.* 274–232 B.C.), was the grandson of Chandragupta Maurya, founder of the Mauryan dynasty. Paucity of historical records makes it difficult to reconstruct the careers and personalities of even the most prominent figures of Indian history. The establishment of Chandragupta's empire (322 B.C.) coincides with the death of Alexander the Great (323 B.C.), and fragments of an account of Chandragupta's court and administration written by Megathenes, ambassador of Seleucus, survive in the writings of Greek and Roman historians. The earliest accounts of Aśoka's reign, on the contrary, are found in legends recorded by Buddhist chroniclers in Ceylon and India. Aśoka, however, left a record which he hoped would endure forever. It is a record inscribed on stone, not as a monument to himself or to commemorate his exploits, but as a record of moral law, of the experience which led him to promulgate it, and the meditations which yield his interpretation and instruction. He refers to the inscriptions sometimes as records of morality (*Dharma-lipi*), sometimes as proclamations of morality (*Dharma-śrāvaṇa*), and he expressed the hope that they would endure in order to provide inspiration and guidance to his descendants and to the people.

The records have survived. They did not, however, serve as a guide to Aśoka's descendants, since the Mauryan dynasty ended about fifty years after his death; nor did they serve as a guide to conduct, since they became indecipherable when Prākrit ceased to be the spoken dialect of the people, and early traditions concerning Aśoka have little bearing on the contents of the inscriptions. The two famous Chinese Buddhist pilgrims who visited India, Fa Hien (A.D. 401–10) and Hiuen Tsang (or Yuan Chwang—A.D. 629–45), describe the remains of Aśoka's palace and other buildings, but their accounts are colored by the legends and indicate no familiarity with the Edicts. Fa Hien saw six pillars. Hiuen Tsang mentions fifteen; some few—four or five—have been conjecturally identified with existing pillars; some have disappeared. Aśoka erected both uninscribed and inscribed pillars, and only two of the inscribed pillars now known have been positively identified with those reported by Hiuen Tsang. The pillars erected at Meerut and Tōprā were transported to Delhi by Sultan Diruz Shah (1351–88). The pillar erected at Kauśāmbī was transported to Allahabad, possibly by Akbar. For the most part, however, with the change of population centers and the encroachment of the jungle, the inscriptions disappeared, and their very location was forgotten.

Knowledge of the Edicts of Aśoka is consequently a recent acquisition. The first modern account of a pillar inscription was set down by Father Tieffenthaler, a Roman Catholic priest who inspected fragments of the Meerut pillar at Delhi in 1756. The Aśoka script was deciphered for the first time by James Prinsep in 1837. Since that time the inscriptions have been rediscovered, published, and interpreted. In a sense, the character of the man who issued the Edicts emerges clearly and sharply: wisdom combined with practical shrewdness; tolerance—unique in his time and unsurpassed by later potentates of like power—combined with moral discrimination and administrative judgment; a concern with the material welfare and happiness of his people combined with a desire to improve their moral outlook and to turn their attention away from the pursuit of material possessions, prestige, and pleasure; a sense of the kinship of all men and a respect for all living creatures combined with a conviction that men must pursue their ends in different ways and peoples must live in peace with each other. Nonetheless, the very uniqueness of the Edicts has tempted interpreters to stress aspects and to draw analogies which make Aśoka seem another religious missionary, sectarian prince, empire-builder and administrator, or philosopher king. His differences from each of these prototypes are no less important than the similarities that have been observed.

The early legends of Aśoka's career have continued to influence the interpretation of the Edicts, in spite of the fact that the incidents they recount and the character they construct are for the most part inconsistent with the Edicts and without independent historical evidence or plausibility. They tell a tale of the conversion to Buddhism of a cruel young tyrant, guilty of unspeakable atrocities, including the murder of ninety-nine of his one hundred brothers, and his subsequent zeal for the spread of Buddhism, both in India and in Ceylon, as a result of which he ceased to be known as Aśoka the Wicked and was called instead the king of Dharma (*Dharmarāja*). The edicts tell of Aśoka's conversion and his becoming a lay disciple; but he appears less as the missionary for one faith than as the exponent of tolerance for all faiths, and his zeal for Buddhism takes the form of calling the attention of Buddhists to the importance of studying Dharma and of avoiding disrupting dissensions.

He has been compared to David and Solomon, kings of Israel; but he did not, like David, wage a series of wars against his neighbors, organize an army and an administration, or introduce innovations in divine worship, such as music and psalmody; he was not, like Solomon, a poet, with a taste for wealth and luxury, nor does he seem to have had Solomon's genius for the development of commerce. He has been compared with Khalif Omar, who had first opposed Islam and was later converted; but Omar made the first collection of the Koran and organized a military-religious commonwealth on the basis of conquest. Constantine the Great issued the Edict of

The Edicts of Aśoka

Milan in 313, by which Christianity was recognized by the Roman Empire, and he convened the first Council of Nicaea, but there is no reason to suppose that these actions resulted from a new moral insight and little indication to suggest that his conversion influence his conduct—and indeed he was not baptized until the time of his death in 337. Moreover, Christianity was established in the Roman Empire, while Buddhism was expelled from India.

Along another line of analogy, the names of other great emperors, like Hammurabi, Charlemagne, and Akbar, have been linked with that of Aśoka. Hammurabi's Code, inscribed on a diorite column about 2100 B.C., was discovered in 1901 in Susa; but the Babylonian code is a system of law, whereas Aśoka proclaimed a moral system which modified existing law and its administration. Charlemagne enlarged and consolidated the kingdom of the Franks, was crowned emperor of the Romans, and became a patron of letters; Akbar enlarged and consolidated the Mogul empire in India, reformed civil administration and the legal system, and enforced toleration of religious diversity.

These comparisons are supplemented by the analogy of the Platonic philosopher-king and of Marcus Aurelius; but Plato specified that the republic ruled by his philosopher-kings never did exist and never would, while Aśoka, whose philosophy was limited to moral meditation, adapted his Edicts to a real, diverse, and imperfect empire; and Marcus Aurelius seems to have used his stoic philosophy for consolation in the stress of political administration, while Aśoka's moral law was a rule not only for himself but for his subordinates and his people. One final analogy is suggested between the careers of Aśoka and Gandhi. They awakened the Indian people, in different periods of history, to make a united effort to pursue the path of peace. Aśoka was called "The Benevolent One"; Gandhi was called "The Great Soul." Both sought to spiritualize statecraft and politics; both were inspired by an ideal of non-violence; both represent a humanism and cultural tradition which has a profound concern for good will and fellowship. But Gandhi avoided political office to carry out his mission, and Aśoka discovered his mission in the exercise of supreme power and expressed it in official proclamations.

When one turns to the Edicts, they speak for themselves despite the distortions of legend and the distractions of analogy. They present a remarkably sharp picture, within limitations, of the man who issued them and the empire he ruled. Moreover, the problems they raise, the objectives they state, and the measures they promulgate have a universality that extends beyond their time and place. They have a particular significance and relevance for the world today. Their larger implications, however, can be

6   *The Edicts of Aśoka*

judged only after they are understood in their historical circumstances.

The Edicts are classified according to the surfaces on which they have been inscribed—rocks, pillars, and caves. These different surfaces, however, were suited to different purposes, and therefore the locations and the contents of the kinds of Edicts follow a pattern. The Rock Edicts are placed along the borders of the empire, including the two Kaliṅga Edicts in the newly conquered territory on the Bay of Bengal. The Fourteen Rock Edicts cover a very large scope, opening with two Edicts on specific provisions concerning the slaughtering of animals and the provision of medical and welfare service; then proceeding to the consideration of broader applications of Dharma in morality and the administration of justice, the nature of Dharma, and its effects in tolerance, ritual, and charity; and closing with the history of the Kaliṅga war and its effects, and the statement of the relations among the Edicts with which this edition opens. The two Kaliṅga Edicts substitute for three Edicts (XI on charity and the kinship of mankind, XII on religious tolerance, and XIII on the Kaliṅga war and the change of heart) two Edicts addressed to the officials administering the conquered territory concerning the problems of morality, the administration of justice, and the problem of reducing the apprehensions of neighboring peoples and promoting international peace. The Pillar Edicts were erected in important cities and along roads within the empire. Three of the pillars are found on the road from Pāṭaliputra, Aśoka's capital city, to the Buddhist holy places at the foot of the Himalayas. The pattern of their contents is simpler: they open with two Edicts on the nature of Dharma, proceed to three which apply Dharma to the control of sin and passion, the promulgation of morality and justice, and the regulation of feasts and animal slaughter, and close with an Edict (or two Edicts in the case of the Tōprā column) on means of promulgating morality. The Minor Rock Edicts are for the most part concentrated in the south and central parts of the empire. They are concerned with Aśoka's activity as a Buddhist lay disciple, with a practical code of ethics, and finally, in the only edict addressed to the Buddhist clergy, Minor Rock Edict III, with Buddhist texts on Dharma.

Two of the three Minor Pillar Edicts and the two Pillar Inscriptions (in Nepal) are concerned with Buddhism. The Cave Inscriptions, found in the Barābar Hills, are brief dedications of shelter for monks during the rainy season.

The Fourteen Rock Edicts are found inscribed in six different localities; eleven of the fourteen plus two additional Edicts (sometimes called Edicts XV and XVI, sometimes the Kaliṅga Edicts) in the place of the missing three (Edicts XI, XII, and XIII) are found at two localities. Two of the sites of the Fourteen

The Edicts of Aśoka

Rock Edicts are near the Western boundaries of the empire on the Arabian Sea at Sōpārā in Bombay State and at Girnar in Saurahtra; two are near the northwest border at Mansehra and Shahbazgarhi in West Pakistan; one is in the north at Kālsī in Uttar Pradesh; one in the south at Erragudi in Andhra Pradesh. The two sites of the eleven Rock Edicts and the Kaliṅga Edicts are near the east coast on the Bay of Bengal at Dhauli and Jaugada in Orissa. In addition to these sixteen Rock Edicts, another, known as Minor Rock Edict I, has been found in seven places in north India and Hyderabad—at Bairāṭ in Rajasthan, Gavīmath, Maskī, and Pālkīguṇḍu in Hyderabad, Gujarrā in Vindhya Pradesh, Rūpnāth in Madhya Pradesh and Sahasrām in Bihar. The same Edict together with a second, known as Minor Rock Edict II, has been found in five places in the south—at Brahmagiri, Jaṭiṅga-Rāmeśvara, and Siddāpura in Mysore and at Erragudi and Rājula-Maṇḍagiri in Andhra. In addition to Minor Rock Edict I, another, known as Minor Rock Edict III, has been found at Bairāṭ. The rocks on which these Edicts have been inscribed are ordinary boulders, chosen for their size and prominence. They are in varying stages of deterioration, and the inscriptions are more or less mutilated by flaking of rock surfaces, exposure to the elements, and wear from human contact of various kinds, including attrition caused by sitting on them. In the case of the Sōpārā inscriptions, thus, only fragments of Rock Edicts VIII and IX survive. The texts used in translation are taken sometimes from one site, sometimes from another, depending on the state of preservation, and missing parts can sometimes be supplied from texts found at other sites.

The Pillar Edicts are a series of six Edicts inscribed on monolithic pillars which have been found in five places—at Meerut (transported to Delhi in the fourteenth century) and Kauśāmbī (transported to Allahabad at an unknown date) in Uttar Pradesh and at Lauriyā-Araraj, Lauriyā-Nandangarh, and Rāmpurvā in Bihar. A sixth pillar, inscribed with a seventh Edict as well as those found on the other pillars, was erected at Tōprā in East Punjab and was transported to Delhi in the fourteenth century. The texts of the six Edicts are almost identical, but in many parts the inscription is incomplete or difficult to decipher. The Allahabad Pillar, which was originally erected at Kauśāmbī (modern Kōsam), is inscribed with two additional Edicts. The first, which is sometimes called Minor Pillar Edict I, is also found at Sānchī in Bhopal State and at Sārnāth in Uttar Pradesh. The inscription is badly preserved in all three places, and there is considerable variation in the texts. The Sārnāth Pillar is inscribed with a further Edict, or a continuation of the first, which is sometimes called Minor Pillar Edict II. The second additional Edict on the Allahabad-Kōsam Pillar, sometimes called Minor Pillar Edict III, commemorates a gift from one of Aśoka's queens, and it is therefore more generally known as the Queen's Edict. Finally, two pillar inscriptions have been found in Nepal, one near the temple of Rummindei, the birthplace of the Buddha, the other near a large tank (pond) called Nigālī Sāgar, where the remains of Kanakamuni, who is counted among the former Buddhas, are enshrined. Aśoka also erected many uninscribed pillars, but, as in the case of the Edict pillars, only a small number has survived. The inscriptions on many of the pillars are difficult to decipher, but the pillars themselves are striking in appearance: their shafts are highly polished with a characteristic Mauryan finish, the formula of which has been lost; they are monoliths, usually about forty or fifty feet high; many are still surmounted with carved capitals—a lion (Lauriyā-Nandangarh), a bell capital surmounted by a lion, the four lions now frequently used as a symbol of India (Sāñchī and Sārnāth), a bell capital (Rummindei)—while some of the uninscribed pillars are surmounted by an elephant or a bull.

The Cave Edicts are found in three of the four caves carved in the granite of the Barābar Hills in Bihar; the fourth contains an inscription from the fifth century A.D. Two of the three Aśoka inscriptions dedicate the caves as dwelling places for the monks of the Ājīvika sect, established by Gośāla, a religious leader contemporary with the Buddha. Three other caves, in another part of the Barābar Hills known as

Nagarjuni Hill, also contain inscriptions. They, too, dedicate the caves to the Ājīvika monks in the name of a monarch who calls himself the "Beloved of the Gods," but these dedications were made by Aśoka's grandson Daśaratha.

All the Edicts, except the Queen's Edict and some of the variants of the Minor Edicts, are published in this edition. They have been arranged under six headings in a sequence intended to introduce the reader, first, to Aśoka's description of the Edicts, then, in turn, to his account of their occasion, his purpose, the means he employed, and, finally, to his interpretation of the nature of Dharma and his specification of its applications. Four of the Edicts have been divided into parts to fit the sequence of this development, but apart from that, the Edicts have been translated as units. If the arrangement serves to facilitate a first appreciation of the Edicts, it will have served its purpose. It should not stand in the way of a clear impression of the form in which they originally appeared or of their place in the sequence of Edicts on rocks and pillars. The following tabulation will assist the reader to relate the order of the inscriptions to the order in which the Edicts appear in this translation.

The Rock Edicts	Place in This Edition
I	VI. B. 1. Applications of Dharma in restrictions on feasts and on the slaughtering of animals

The inscriptions are written in Prākrit, the vernacular language of Magadha, not in Sanskrit, the literary language. The style is simple and at times even crude. It has been argued therefore that the words of the inscriptions were probably those actually used by the emperor, that they probably differ from the official language of the administration, and that they were probably intelligible to the common people throughout Aśoka's empire. Prākrit forms the connecting link between Sanskrit and the modern Indo-European languages of India. Its use as a spoken language was widespread in Aśoka's time, and it appears on the bilingual coins of the Greek kings of Bactria. Two scripts or alphabets are used—Kharoṣṭhī in the northwestern corner of the empire, Brāhmī elsewhere in the empire. The Kharoṣṭhī alphabet fell into disuse centuries ago, but the Brāhmī alphabet is the source of all the alphabets of the Sanskritic and Dravidian languages of modern India as well as of other alphabets of southeast Asia. Since many of the Edicts are addressed to the people, the inscriptions have been taken as evidence for a high degree of literacy among Aśoka's subjects. Whatever the proportion of those who could read the inscriptions themselves, however, the choice of language is a sign of the universality of Aśoka's conception of morality. It was not a recondite ideal to be pursued by speculative philosophers, systematic theologians, or contemplative mystics; it was an attitude of mind and a way of life for all men.

Several of the Edicts indicate the dates of their promulgation relative to other events, such as Aśo-

ka's coronation and his becoming a lay disciple. It is
easy to establish a relative sequence in the promulgation of the Edicts (but not necessarily in the dates of
particular inscriptions, since Aśoka gave instructions that the edicts should be copied and inscribed
wherever there were stones or pillars available), and
a conjectural chronology of his reign can be constructed on that sequence. The first Minor Edict
records that he had been energetic in the performance
of his duties as lay disciple for two and a half years.
Rock Edict XIII dates the Kalinga war eight years
after his coronation. Rock Edict VIII places his visit
to Sambodhi ten years after his coronation and marks
that visit as the first of his Dharma tours. Rock Edicts
III and IV were issued twelve years after his coronation. Rock Edict V records the creation of the post of
officers in charge of morality (*Dharma-mahāmātras*)
thirteen years after his coronation, and the inscription
could not therefore have been made before that year.
The first two cave inscriptions are dated twelve years
after his coronation, the third, nineteen years. Pillar
Edicts I, IV, V, and VI were promulgated twenty-six
years after Aśoka's coronation; Pillar Edict VII, twenty-seven years. According to the tradition of the
Purāṇas and the Pali books, his reign lasted thirty-
six or thirty-seven years. The time of Aśoka's birth
is put at about 304 B.C. His accession to the throne
probably occurred no later than 274 B.C. and his
coronation no later than 270 B.C. The Kalinga war

then took place about 262 B.C. He was probably converted to Buddhism earlier, and his increased devotion probably dated from about the time of the war. The Dharma tours were inaugurated about 260 B.C., and Minor Rock Edicts I and II (and possibly III) were issued the same year. These were the first of the edicts. The Kalinga Edicts (Rock Edicts XV and XVI) may have been published in 259 B.C., but the Fourteen Rock Edicts were issued and two of the caves in the Barābar Hills were dedicated about 258–257 B.C. The officers in charge of Dharma were inaugurated in 257 B.C. The two commemorative pillars in Nepal were erected about 250 B.C. The Pillar Edicts were then erected in 243–242 B.C. The date of Aśoka's death is sometimes set at 237–236 B.C. and sometimes at 232 B.C., depending on whether the thirty-six or thirty-seven years of his reign are calculated from the time of his accession or of his coronation.

Aśoka's career turns on one important event, his only military campaign—the short Kalinga war in which he conquered a neighboring people. He records his profound emotion in reaction to the cruelties of this war and his "change of heart." According to the testimony of the Edicts, the change was manifested in his personal life, in the operation of the royal household, and in the organization of governmental administration. The Edicts, which are a consequence as well as an expression of the change, relate it in all its dimensions to the idea of Dharma, of

The Edicts of Aśoka

morality—Dharma provides a code of personal conduct, a bond of human relations and political justice, and a principle of international relations, and Dharma turns the lives of men away from evil deeds, mutual intolerance, and armed conflict.

In the new career on which Aśoka embarked, the religious, political, and moral motivations and objectives are inseparably interrelated—religious observance and political administration are transformed by application of moral principles, and ethics is made concrete and relevant to everyday action and feeling. Aśoka's conversion to Buddhism, or at least his increase in zeal as a lay disciple, coincided approximately with the events of the Kaliṅga war. His mission became study of Dharma, action according to Dharma, and inculcation of Dharma. Since Dharma is a fundamental concept in Buddhism, this concern for Dharma has been interpreted—in the spirit of the legends, which contain no account of the Kaliṅga war and its effect but do set forth the efforts of Aśoka to spread Buddhism and the missions of his son Mahendra and his grandson Sumana to Ceylon—as a missionary zeal for Buddhism. However, Dharma was also a fundamental idea of Hinduism and of the other sects of India. Far from restricting Dharma to the tenets and practices of a single religion, Aśoka asserts in Rock Edict XII that Dharma is cultivated in all religions and sects, and he seeks to advance Dharma in all men whatever their religious affiliations;

and, true to this purpose, he instructs Buddhists, in Minor Rock Edict III, to pay more attention to Buddhist texts on Dharma. Rock Edict VII presents the ideal of tolerant harmony among all the sects of his dominion. The newly created officers of Dharma were charged to attend to the welfare of all his subjects, including special functions in each of the sects, Hindu, Ājīvika, and Jain as well as Buddhist. Finally, foreign missions, which were dispatched not only to Ceylon but to the five Hellenistic Greek kingdoms ranging from Syria to Macedonia, are mentioned in two Edicts—Rock Edict XIII records that these peoples received instruction in Dharma, Rock Edict II that they received medical services. Dharma and welfare are closely connected in the Edicts, and the tone and spirit of the Edicts suggests that the measures referred to were designed to improve the material and spiritual conditions of the peoples of neighboring states rather than to convert them to Buddhism. The cultivation of Dharma was to emphasize morality in religion, in man's relations with the gods, in his conception of sacraments, in his relations with other men, in his charity. One short inscription in Greek and Aramaic—an edict prohibiting the slaughter of animals similar in purport to Rock Edict I—has recently been found at Kandahar in Afghanistan. Kandahar was within Aśoka's empire, part of the territory ceded to his grandfather by Seleucus Nicator, but the inscription lends plausibility to Aśoka's claim to influence in the Hellenistic Greek kingdoms and illustrates vividly the extent to which his instructions were carried out to inscribe the Edicts wherever possible.

In much the same fashion, Aśoka used the idea of Dharma to reorganize the administration of the empire. His accession to the throne was not unopposed, and the empire was vast in extent and divided into many sects, classes, and castes—referred to in the Edicts in expressions like "ascetics and householders" and "rich and poor." Indian rulers were absolute sovereigns limited by social disorder, political intrigue, and military rivalry. Aśoka inherited a system of administration from his grandfather and father. The Edicts were one means by which he laid down fundamental policies interpreting the laws. Subordinate officials were given discretion in their own districts within a system which provided for constant inspection and supervision. A special class of officers was specifically charged with morality or Dharma, and provision was made against unjust imprisonment and undue torture and for appeal before the execution of sentence. The functions of the officials were extended to include provision of medical aid, roads, watering sheds for man and beast, shade trees, and rest houses. The whole political organization was made subsidiary to moral law in a concrete translation of the law into specific forms of human and social relations.

The focus of Aśoka's activities was therefore moral. The morality did not consist in the preachment of an ideal or in the prescriptions of a code. Aśoka taught that the essence of law, religious and political, was insight into oneself and respect for others. The method was instruction, and although instruction depends on prescriptions as well as meditation, he was convinced that prescription was valueless, and he placed all his confidence in what he called meditation. Meditation as he conceived it was not theoretic speculation or mystical contemplation—it manifested itself in one's relations to others and in one's inner attitude and outer aspirations. Its effect was a conversion toward other desires and ideals under the influence of a broader and richer conception of human kinship and dignity, which was to lessen tensions, fears, and covetousness. It adumbrated a new idea of responsibility in which tolerance for others is not indifference but an influence toward improvement. It involves an insight into morality applied in political and social relations which stands in striking contrast to the moral confidence which judges others by one's own standards and the moralizing deception which preaches what no one practices. History provides no information concerning how the program worked out in the administration of Aśoka, but the basic ideas and practices set forth in the Edicts take on a new meaning and relevance in a time like ours when the problems of individuals and of nations are once again fundamentally moral problems.

THE EDICTS

I

THE EDICTS: THEIR ADAPTATION TO CIRCUMSTANCES AND THEIR REPETITIONS

Rock Edict XIV

These edicts on Dharma[1] have been inscribed by the command of King Priyadarśi,[2] Beloved of the Gods. Some of these moral edicts are greatly abridged, some less abridged, and some are inscribed in full.

[1] "Dharma" conveys the associated meanings of "Law" and "morality," with overtones of both religious piety and social obligation. Any single translation would overstress one of these dimensions of meaning at the expense of the others and would suggest dubious analogies with other religious traditions, legal systems, or moral codes. The word "Dharma" has therefore been retained for the most part in this translation, but occasionally, where the context suggests that the emphasis is desirable, it has been translated as "morality." Aśoka makes his own characteristic use of a term which has social, doctrinal, and mystic implications in Hinduism and Buddhism. The retention of the word "Dharma" will permit the reader to reconstruct Aśoka's meaning and to decide for himself to what extent it departs from narrower limitations to open up a new and broader moral insight. For a discussion of the meaning and implications of Dharma, see the Foreword (pp. ix–xvi).

[2] Aśoka never refers to himself simply by that name in the Edicts; it appears in combinations twice in the Edicts. A variety of expressions is employed instead: "Devānāmpriyaḥ Priyadarśi rāja," "Devānāmpriyaḥ," "Devānāmpriyaḥ Aśoka," "Priyadarśi rāja," and "rāja Priyadarśi." Aśoka took these titles when he assumed the throne, and he himself applies them to his predecessors in the Maurya dynasty. In later documents they are also applied to some

All the edicts are not suited to all places, for my dominions are large. Many inscriptions have been made, and I shall command many more to be made.

Some of the edicts have been inscribed again and again because of the charm of the teachings [and in the hope that] men may follow their precepts after hearing them repeatedly.

Some edicts may have been engraved incompletely because parts were unsuited to the place, or because there were reasons for their exclusion, or because of errors on the part of the transcriber.

---

of his contemporaries who ruled in other countries, but there is no conclusive evidence to determine whether they were actually used by the monarchs to which they were applied or were innovations of Aśoka's. They originated as honorific titles and apparently carried little more meaning in use than modern titles like "Majesty," "Eminence," "Highness." Devānāmpriyaḥ, literally, means "beloved of the gods" or "dear to the gods"; Priyadarśī means "one who sees to the good of others," "one who looks with kindness," or, more freely, "the benevolent one"; rājā simply means "a king." Since the titles are honorific, some translators have used expressions like "His Sacred and Gracious Majesty" to refer to Aśoka; others have left the words in Prākrit or in Sanskrit equivalents; still others have translated them literally as "The Beloved of the Gods" and "The Benevolent One." None of these solutions seemed to us to be satisfactory: the modern titles are anachronistic and carry irrelevant connotations; the strangeness and variety of the Prākrit words is distracting to readers unfamiliar with them; the repetition of unaccustomed descriptive titles loses the conventional formality of the titles and intrudes a distracting dimension of meaning. We have therefore translated "Priyadarśī rājā" and "rājā Priyadarśī" "King Priyadarśī" and have used that title for all references to Aśoka, varying it occasionally by adding the epithet "Beloved of the Gods."

THE OCCASION AND THE PURPOSE OF THE EDICTS: THE KALINGA WAR, AŚOKA'S CHANGE OF HEART, AND THE IDEAL OF CONQUEST BY DHARMA

Rock Edict XIII

The Kaliṅga country was conquered by King Priyadarśī, Beloved of the Gods, in the eighth year of his reign. One hundred and fifty thousand persons were carried away captive, one hundred thousand were slain, and many times that number died.

Immediately after the Kaliṅgas had been conquered, King Priyadarśī became intensely devoted to the study of Dharma, to the love of Dharma, and to the inculcation of Dharma.

The Beloved of the Gods, conqueror of the Kaliṅgas, is moved to remorse now. For he has felt profound sorrow and regret because the conquest of a people previously unconquered involves slaughter, death, and deportation.

But there is a more important reason for the King's remorse. The Brāhmaṇas and Śramaṇas [the priestly and ascetic orders][3] as well as the followers of other

[3] "Brāhmaṇas" refers not to the caste but to the Brahmanical orders of ascetics, of which there were many sects; "Śramaṇas" refers to another group of ascetics which likewise was split into many sects. The two combined would include all ascetics, Hindu and Buddhist. The expression is rendered hereafter either "Brahmin and Buddhist ascetics" or simply "priests and ascetics."

The Occasion and Purpose of the Edicts   27

religions and the householders—who all practiced obedience to superiors, parents, and teachers, and proper courtesy and firm devotion to friends, acquaintances, companions, relatives, slaves, and servants—all suffer from the injury, slaughter, and deportation inflicted on their loved ones. Even those who escaped calamity themselves are deeply afflicted by the misfortunes suffered by those friends, acquaintances, companions, and relatives for whom they feel an undiminished affection. Thus all men share in the misfortune, and this weighs on King Priyadarśi's mind.

[Moreover, there is no country except that of the Yōnas (that is, the Greeks) where Brahmin and Buddhist ascetics do not exist] and there is no place where men are not attached to one faith or another.

Therefore, even if the number of people who were killed or who died or who were carried away in the Kaliṅga war had been only one one-hundredth or one one-thousandth of what it actually was, this would still have weighed on the King's mind.

King Priyadarśi now thinks that even a person who wrongs him must be forgiven for wrongs that can be forgiven.

King Priyadarśi seeks to induce even the forest peoples who have come under his dominion [that is, primitive peoples in the remote sections of the conquered territory] to adopt this way of life and this ideal. He reminds them, however, that he exercises the power to punish, despite his repentance, in order to induce them to desist from their crimes and escape execution.

For King Priyadarśi desires security, self-control, impartiality, and cheerfulness for all living creatures.

King Priyadarśi considers moral conquest [that is, conquest by Dharma, *Dharma-vijaya*] the most important conquest. He has achieved this moral conquest repeatedly both here and among the peoples living beyond the borders of his kingdom, even as far away as six hundred *yojanas* [about three thousand miles], where the Yōna [Greek] king Antiyoka rules, and even beyond Antiyoka in the realms of the four kings named Turamaya, Antikini, Maka, and Alikasudara,[4] and to the south among the Cholas and Pāṇḍyas [in the southern tip of the Indian peninsula] as far as Ceylon.

Here in the King's dominion also, among the Yōnas [inhabitants of a northwest frontier province, probably Greeks] and the Kambōjas [neighbors of

---

[4] The five kings referred to have been identified as follows: Antiyoka = Antiochos II Theos of Syria (261–246 B.C.); Turamaya = Ptolemy II Philadelphos of Egypt (285–247 B.C.); Antikini = Antigonos Gonatas of Macedonia (278–239 B.C.); Maka = Magas of Cyrene (300–258 B.C.); and Alikasudara = Alexander of Epirus (272?–258 B.C.). The passage is of extreme importance not only for dating the events of Aśoka's reign but also for judging the extent of communications in his times. It indicates, moreover, the date 258 B.C. as the latest date at which all five could be referred to simultaneously and therefore fixes the approximate date of the edict.

the Yōnas], among the Nābhakas and Nābhapaṅktis [who probably lived along the Himalayan frontier], among the Bhojas and Paitryaṇikas, among the Andhras and Paulindas [all peoples of the Indian peninsula], everywhere people heed his instructions in Dharma.

Even in countries which King Priyadarśī's envoys have not reached, people have heard about Dharma and about his Majesty's ordinances and instructions in Dharma, and they themselves conform to Dharma and will continue to do so.

Wherever conquest is achieved by Dharma, it produces satisfaction. Satisfaction is firmly established by conquest by Dharma [since it generates no opposition of conquered and conqueror]. Even satisfaction, however, is of little importance. King Priyadarśī attaches value ultimately only to consequences of action in the other world.

This edict on Dharma has been inscribed so that my sons and great-grandsons who may come after me should not think new conquests worth achieving. If they do conquer, let them take pleasure in moderation and mild punishments. Let them consider moral conquest the only true conquest.

This is good, here and hereafter. Let their pleasure be pleasure in morality [Dharma-rati]. For this alone is good, here and hereafter.

III

THE OBJECTIVES OF INCULCA-
TION OF DHARMA

Rock Edict IV

For many hundreds of years in the past, slaughter of animals, cruelty to living creatures, discourtesy to relatives, and disrespect for priests and ascetics have been increasing.

But now, because of King Priyadarśi's practice of Dharma, the sound of war drums has become the call to Dharma [rather than to war], summoning the people to exhibitions of the chariots of the gods, elephants, fireworks, and other divine displays.

King Priyadarśi's inculcation of Dharma has increased, beyond anything observed in many hundreds of years, abstention from killing animals and from cruelty to living beings, kindliness in human and family relations, respect for priests and ascetics, and obedience to mother and father and elders.

The practice of Dharma has been promoted in this and other ways. King Priyadarśi will continue to promote the practice of Dharma. His sons, grandsons, and great-grandsons to the end of time will ever promote the practice of Dharma; standing firm themselves in Dharma, they will instruct the people in Dharma and moral conduct.

For instruction in Dharma is the best of actions.

The practice of Dharma is impossible for the immoral man. To increase this practice, even to forestall its diminution, is laudable.

This edict has been inscribed in order to inspire my descendants to work for the promotion and to prevent the decline of Dharma. King Priyadarśi commanded this record to be made twelve years after his coronation.

IV

WAYS TO INCULCATE DHARMA

Pillar Edict VII

King Priyadarśī, the Beloved of the Gods, speaks as follows:

In the past, kings have thought about ways of increasing the people's devotion to Dharma, but the people did not make progress enough in morality.

Concerning this, King Priyadarśī says:

This occurred to me. Since in the past kings have thought about ways of increasing the people's devotion to Dharma, but the people did not make progress enough in morality, how can the people be induced to follow Dharma strictly? How can progress in morality be increased sufficiently? How can I raise them up by the promotion of Dharma?

Pursuing this subject, King Priyadarśī says:

This occurred to me. I shall issue proclamations on Dharma, and I shall order instruction in Dharma to be given to the people. Hearing these proclamations and instructions, the people will conform to Dharma; they will raise themselves up and will make progress by the promotion of Dharma. To this end I have issued proclamations on Dharma, and I have instituted various kinds of moral and religious instruction.

My highest officials, who have authority over large numbers of people, will expound and spread the precepts of Dharma. I have instructed the provincial governors, too, who are in charge of many hundred thousand people, concerning how to guide people devoted to Dharma.

King Priyadarśī says:

Having come to this conclusion, therefore, I have erected pillars proclaiming Dharma. I have appointed officers charged with the spread of Dharma, called *Dharma-mahāmātras*. I have issued proclamations on Dharma.

[There follows a section concerning the rest houses, watering sheds, and trees provided for travelers; it is found below in Section VI. B. 3. Aśoka continues by detailing the duties of his Censors of Morality.]

King Priyadarśī says:

My officers charged with the spread of Dharma are occupied with various kinds of services beneficial to ascetics and householders, and they are empowered to concern themselves with all sects. I have ordered some of them to look after the affairs of the Saṁgha [the Buddhist religious orders], some to take care of the Brahmin and Ajīvika ascetics, some to work among the Nirgranthas [the Jaina monks], and some among the various other religious sects. Different

34   *The Edicts of Aśoka*

officials are thus assigned specifically to the affairs of different religions, but my officers for spreading Dharma are occupied with all sects.

King Priyadarśī says:

These and many other high officials take care of the distribution of gifts from myself as well as from the queens. They report in various ways to all my harem worthy recipients of charity, both here [at Pāṭaliputra] and in the provinces. I also ordered some of them to supervise the distribution of gifts from my sons and the sons of other queens, in order [to promote] noble deeds of Dharma and conformity to the precepts of Dharma. These noble deeds and this conformity [consist in] promoting compassion, liberality, truthfulness, purity, gentleness, and goodness.

King Priyadarśī says:

Whatever good deeds I have done the people have imitated, and they have followed them as a model. In doing so, they have progressed and will progress in obedience to parents and teachers, in respect for elders, in courtesy to priests and ascetics, to the poor and distressed, and even to slaves and servants.

[There follows a section on meditation and non-violence; it is found below in Section V. 1. Pillar Edict VII then concludes with a statement of the moral uses of the enduring quality of inscriptions.]

This edict on Dharma has been inscribed in order that it may endure and be followed as long as [my] sons and great-grandsons [shall reign and] as long as the sun and moon [shall shine]. For one who adheres to it will attain happiness in this world and hereafter. I ordered this edict inscribed twenty-seven years after my coronation.

Concerning this edict on Dharma, King Priyadarśī says:

This edict on morality should be engraved wherever stone pillars or stone slabs are available, in order that it may endure forever.

Pillar Edict VI

King Priyadarśī says:

Twelve years after my coronation I ordered edicts on Dharma to be inscribed for the welfare and happiness of the people, in order that they might give up their former ways of life and grow in Dharma in the particular respects set forth.

Since I am convinced that the welfare and happiness of the people will be achieved only in this way, I consider how I may bring happiness to the people, not only to relatives of mine or residents of my capital city, but also to those who are far removed from me. I act in the same manner with respect to all.

I am concerned similarly with all classes.

Moreover, I have honored all religious sects with various offerings. But I consider it my principal duty to visit [the people] personally.

I commanded this edict on Dharma to be inscribed twenty-six years after my coronation.

The Edicts of Aśoka

2. AŚOKA'S PARTICIPATION IN THE PROGRAM AS ADMINISTRATOR AND AS EXAMPLE

Rock Edict VIII

In the past, kings[5] used to go on pleasure tours (*vihār-yātrās*). On these tours, they hunted and indulged in other pastimes.

King Priyadarśī, however, became enlightened in wisdom (*saṁbuddha*) ten years after his coronation. Since then his tours have been moral-tours (*Dharma-yātrās*).

He visits priests and ascetics and makes gifts to them; he visits the aged and gives them money; he visits the people of rural areas, instructing them in Dharma and discussing it with them.

King Priyadarśī takes great pleasure in these tours, far more than could result from other tours.

Rock Edict VI

King Priyadarśī says:

In the past, state business was not transacted or reports made at all hours of the day. I have therefore made arrangements that officials may have access to me and may report on the affairs of my people at all times and in all places—when I am eating, when I am in the harem or my inner apartments, when I am at-

---

[5] Aśoka here applies the expression "Beloved of the Gods" to his predecessors, calling them *Devānāmpriyaḥ*.

tending to the cattle, when I am walking or engaged in religious exercises. I now attend to the affairs of the people in all places. And when a donation or a proclamation that I have ordered verbally, or an urgent matter which I have delegated to my high officials, causes a debate or dispute in the Council, this must be reported to me immediately, at all hours and in all places. These are my orders.

I am never completely satisfied with my work or my vigilance in carrying out public affairs. I consider the promotion of the people's welfare my highest duty, and its exercise is grounded in work and constant application.

No task is more important to me than promoting the well-being of all the people. Such work as I accomplish contributes to discharging the debt I owe to all living creatures to make them happy in this world and to help them attain heaven in the next.

I have ordered this edict on Dharma inscribed in order that it may endure forever and in order that my sons, grandsons, and great-grandsons may follow it for the welfare of all. This is difficult to do, however, without devoted and sustained work.

Rock Edict V

King Priyadarśi says:

It is difficult to do a good deed. He who performs a good deed accomplishes a difficult task. Nevertheless, I have performed many good deeds. If my sons,

The Edicts of Aśoka

grandsons, and descendants to the end of time follow my example, they will do well. But he who neglects even a part of this command does evil. For evil is easily committed.

[The Edict continues with a statement of the duties of officials charged with the promotion of morality; it is found below in Section VI. B. 2.]

Rock Edict X

King Priyadarśi does not consider glory or renown of great value except in so far as the people, at present and in the future, hear of his practice of Dharma and live in accordance with Dharma. For this purpose he desires glory and fame.

[The concluding section of the edict elaborates the use of Dharma in avoiding sin; it is found below in Section VI. A. 1.]

V

THE NATURE OF DHARMA

I. AS MEDITATION AND NON-VIOLENCE

Pillar Edict VII [continued from IV. 1]

King Priyadarśi says:

The people can be induced to advance in Dharma by only two means, by moral prescriptions and by meditation. Of the two, moral prescriptions are of little consequence, but meditation is of great importance. The moral prescriptions I have promulgated include rules making certain animals inviolable, and many others. But even in the case of abstention from injuring and from killing living creatures, it is by meditation that people have progressed in Dharma most.

Pillar Edict II

King Priyadarśī says:

Dharma is good. But what does Dharma consist of? It consists of few sins and many good deeds, of kindness, liberality, truthfulness, and purity.

I have bestowed even the gift of sight [i.e., spiritual insight] on men in various ways. I have decreed many kindnesses, including even the grant of life, to living creatures, two-footed and four-footed as well as birds and aquatic animals. I have also performed many other good deeds.

I have ordered this edict on Dharma to be inscribed in order that people may act according to it and that it may endure for a long time. And he who follows it completely will do good deeds.

Pillar Edict I

King Priyardarśī says:

I commanded this edict on Dharma to be engraved twenty-six years after my coronation.

It is difficult to achieve happiness, either in this world or in the next, except by intense love of Dharma, intense self-examination, intense obedience, intense fear [of sin], and intense enthusiasm. Yet as a result of my instruction, regard for Dharma and love of Dharma have increased day by day and will continue to increase.

The Nature of Dharma   41

My officials of all ranks—high, low, and intermediate—act in accordance with the precepts of my instruction, and by their example and influence they are able to recall fickle-minded people to their duty. The officials of the border districts enforce my injunctions in the same way. For these are their rules: to govern according to Dharma, to administer justice according to Dharma, to advance the people's happiness according to Dharma, and to protect them according to Dharma.

Brahmagiri Rock Edict II

King Priyadarśī says:

One should obey one's father and mother. One should respect the supreme value and sacredness of life. One should speak the truth. One should practice these virtues of Dharma.

In the same way, pupils should honor their teachers, and in families one should behave with fitting courtesy to relatives. This is the traditional rule of Dharma, and it is conducive to long life. Men should act according to it.

Written by Chapaḍa the Scribe.

4. AS CHARITY AND THE KIN-
SHIP OF MANKIND

Rock Edict XI

King Priyadarśī says:

There is no gift that can equal the gift of Dharma,
the establishment of human relations on Dharma, the
distribution of wealth through Dharma, or kinship in
Dharma.[6]

[6] In these four concepts Aśoka makes use once more of a device
which he employs throughout the Edicts to define his idea of
Dharma—the combination of the term "Dharma" with a term
applied to customary human activities in order to transform customary practice by association with a moral ideal. Thus, contact
with war and conquest led him to the idea of *Dharma-vijaya*, conquest by Dharma, which is the only true conquest and which re-
duces all true pleasures to *Dharma-rati*, pleasure in Dharma. The
practice of pleasure tours led him to the idea of *Dharma-yātrās*,
moral tours which yield greater fulfilment and pleasure than
rounds of amusement. Religious observance is associated with
charity and almsgiving, which Aśoka practices and encourages provided it does not degenerate into an automatic substitute for the
recognition of moral responsibility. True charity is *Dharma-dāna*,
the gift of Dharma, and it carries with it the ideas of *Dharma-
saṁstava*, acquaintance with other men and relations with them in
Dharma; *Dharma-saṁvibhāga*, the distribution of riches in Dharma;
and *Dharma-saṁbandha*, kinship in Dharma. In the following
Edict (Rock Edict IX) Aśoka uses the same device to clarify the
idea of religious ritual and ceremonials, holding that all ceremonies
are of doubtful value except *Dharma-maṅgala*, the ceremony of
Dharma. The effect in each case is the same: to transform war,
social relations, political administration, religious practices, by refer-
ring them to the fundamental moral principles which at once

That gift consists in proper treatment of slaves and servants, obedience to mother and father, liberality to friends, acquaintances, relatives, priests and ascetics, and abstention from the slaughter of animals.

Father, son, brother, master, friend, acquaintance, or even neighbor ought to say, "This has merit. This ought to be done."

If one acts in this way, one achieves by the gift of Dharma happiness in this world and infinite merit in the world to come.

---

reveal the degradation, insensitivity, and cruelty of current practices and substitute for them simple maxims and clear guides.

Rock Edict IX

King Priyadarśi, the Beloved of the Gods, says:

People perform various ceremonies. Among the occasions on which ceremonies are performed are sicknesses, marriages of sons or daughters, children's births, and departures on journeys. Women in particular have recourse to many diverse, trivial, and meaningless ceremonies.

It is right that ceremonies be performed. But this kind bears little fruit. The ceremony of Dharma (*Dharma-mangala*), on the contrary, is very fruitful. It consists in proper treatment of slaves and servants, reverence to teachers, restraint of violence toward living creatures, and liberality to priests and ascetics. These and like actions are called the ceremonies of Dharma.

Therefore, a father, son, brother, master, friend, acquaintance, or even neighbor ought to say about such actions, "These are good; they should be performed until their purpose is achieved. I shall observe them."

Other ceremonies are of doubtful value. They may achieve their purpose, or they may not. Moreover the purposes for which they are performed are limited to this world.

The ceremony of Dharma, on the other hand, is

not limited to time. Even if it does not achieve its object in this world, it produces unlimited merit in the next world. But if it produces its object in this world, it achieves both effects: the purpose desired in this world and unlimited merit in the next.

It has also been said that liberality is commendable. But there is no greater liberality than the gift of Dharma or the benefit of Dharma. Therefore, a friend, well-wisher, relative, or companion should urge one when the occasion arises, saying, "You should do this; this is commendable. By doing this you may attain heaven." And what is more worth doing than attaining heaven?[7]

[7] This paragraph appears in the Girnār, Dhauli, and Jaugaḍa texts of the Rock Edicts as a substitute for the two preceding paragraphs.

VI

APPLICATIONS OF DHARMA

A. Universal Manifestations

1. AGAINST SINS AND PASSIONS IN THE INDIVIDUAL

Pillar Edict III

King Priyadarśī says:

A man notices only his worthy actions, thinking to himself, "This is a good deed that I have done." He does not notice his sins, thinking, "This is an evil deed that I have done; this is what is called a sin." Such self-scrutiny and insight are difficult.

Nonetheless, a man must say to himself, "Ferocity, cruelty, anger, arrogance, and jealousy lead to sin; I must not let myself be ruined by these passions." He should make a clear distinction among actions, saying, "This action is directed to my good in this world and that other to my good in the world to come."

Rock Edict X [continued from IV. 2]

Whatever effort King Priyadarśī makes is for the sake of the life hereafter and in order that men may be saved from enslavement. For sin is enslavement.

Rich and poor alike will find it difficult to do this unless they make a great effort and renounce all other aims. It is more difficult for the rich to do this than for the poor.

2. AGAINST IRRELIGION IN THE INDIVIDUAL

Maskī Rock Edict

[The edict opens with Aśoka's statement of his adherence to Buddhism; it is found below in Section VI. B. 4. The edict then continues with an expression of his conviction that religious experience is accessible to poor and rich alike, in terms which recall his statements about avoiding sin and passions in Rock Edict X.]

In Jambudvīpa, the gods who formerly had no relations with men have now been associated with them.[8] But this result which I have achieved is within

[8] This Edict appears in twelve inscriptions with some variations in the text. Some texts assert that men who were "unmingled with the gods" had come to be "mingled with the gods"; two (the Rūpnāth and Maskī inscriptions) speak of the gods as having been unmingled. This difference has led to a difference of translation: those who emphasize the first form interpret the statement to mean that men in Jambudvīpa have been brought back to religion as a result of Aśoka's missionary activities; those who emphasize the second interpret it to mean that Aśoka has exerted himself to unite the different sects in a single religion. One text, that at Brahmagiri, which is the only one in which this sentence is intact, does not resolve this dispute, since it may be interpreted to mean either that men have been "mingled with the gods" or that they have been "united along with their gods."

The dispute clearly has its origin in the tendency of later generations of interpreters to claim Aśoka as a great religious leader engaged in the propagation of a faith, Buddhist or Hindu, rather than in any difficulty in the text. Other Edicts are devoted to the imthe power even of a poor man if he is devoted to Dharma. It is incorrect to suppose that it is limited to the rich. Poor and rich should be told, "If you act in this way, this praiseworthy achievement will endure a long time and will be augmented a time and a half."

---

portance of religious toleration and respect for all religions. This is consistent with Aśoka's prohibition in still other Edicts of religious disputes and schisms *within* Buddhism, since the object of his attack in those Edicts is dogmatic controversy which threatens the very essence of religion. In like fashion, the religion which he sought to advance was not adherence to the tenets of a chosen creed, but the practice of Dharma. The point of the Maski Edict, and the other texts which vary from it verbally, is underlined by the fact that Aśoka chose the "men of Jambudvīpa" as his instance of "men unmingled with Gods." Jambudvīpa was not a backwoods region which needed a missionary to introduce religion; it figures in the sacred texts as the country in which the spiritual life was at its highest. Aśoka is therefore saying that even men who spend their lives in religious practices may show no awareness of God, whereas all men, priest and seculars, poor and rich alike, may repeat Aśoka's achievement by discovering Dharma and devoting themselves to moral practices which are the essence of religion.

The notion of gods and men mingling is similar to Cicero's definition of the world (*universus hic mundus*) as a commonwealth of gods and men (*De legibus* i. 7. 23). For Cicero this means that men and gods share the same virtues and the same law.

The Edicts of Aśoka

3 · AGAINST RELIGIOUS INTOLERANCE AND DISCRIMINATION WITHIN THE COMMUNITY

Rock Edict VII

King Priyadarśi wishes members of all faiths to live everywhere in his kingdom.

For they all seek mastery of the senses and purity of mind. Men are different in their inclinations and passions, however, and they may perform the whole of their duties or only part.

Even if one is not able to make lavish gifts, mastery of the senses, purity of mind, gratitude, and steadfast devotion are commendable and essential.

Rock Edict XII

King Priyadarśi honors men of all faiths, members of religious orders and laymen alike, with gifts and various marks of esteem. Yet he does not value either gifts or honors as much as growth in the qualities essential to religion in men of all faiths.

This growth may take many forms, but its root is in guarding one's speech to avoid extrolling one's own faith and disparaging the faith of others improperly or, when the occasion is appropriate, immoderately.

The faiths of others all deserve to be honored for one reason or another. By honoring them, one exalts one's own faith and at the same time performs a service to the faith of others. By acting otherwise, one injures one's own faith and also does disservice to that of others. For if a man extols his own faith and disparages another because of devotion to his own and because he wants to glorify it, he seriously injures his own faith.

Therefore concord alone is commendable, for through concord men may learn and respect the conception of Dharma accepted by others.

King Priyadarśī desires men of all faiths to know each other's doctrines and to acquire sound doctrines. Those who are attached to their particular faiths should be told that King Priyadarśī does not value gifts or honors as much as growth in the qualities essential to religion in men of all faiths.

Many officials are assigned to tasks bearing on this purpose—the officers in charge of spreading Dharma, the superintendents of women in the royal household, the inspectors of cattle and pasture lands, and other officials.

The objective of these measures is the promotion of each man's particular faith and the glorification of Dharma.

4. AGAINST AGGRESSION AND TENSION BETWEEN STATES

Kaliṅga Edict II

King Priyadarśī says:

I command that the following instructions be communicated to my officials at Samāpā:[9]

Whenever something right comes to my attention, I want it put into practice and I want effective means devised to achieve it. My principal means to do this is to transmit my instructions to you.

All men are my children. Just as I seek the welfare and happiness of my own children in this world and the next, I seek the same things for all men.

Unconquered peoples along the borders of my dominions may wonder what my disposition is toward them. My only wish with respect to them is that they should not fear me, but trust me; that they should expect only happiness from me, not misery; that they should understand further that I will forgive them for offenses which can be forgiven; that they should be induced by my example to practice Dharma; and that they should attain happiness in this world and the next.

I transmit these instructions to you in order to dis-

[9] The inscription at Jaugaḍa is addressed to the officials at Samāpā, the Dhauli text to "the prince and the officials at Tosalī." The two cities were the headquarters of the Jagauda and Dhauli districts of the Kaliṅga country.

charge my debt [to them] by instructing you and making known to you my will and my unshakable resolution and commitment. You must perform your duties in this way and establish their confidence in the King, assuring them that he is like a father to them, that he loves them as he loves himself, and that they are like his own children.

Having instructed you and informed you of my will and my unshakable resolution and commitment, I will appoint officials to carry out this program in all the provinces. You are able to inspire the border peoples with confidence in me and to advance their welfare and happiness in this world and the next. By doing so, you will also attain heaven and help me discharge my debts to the people.

This edict has been inscribed here so that my officials will work at all times to inspire the peoples of neighboring countries with confidence in me and to induce them to practice Dharma.

This edict must be proclaimed every four months [at the beginning of the three seasons—hot, rainy, and cold] on Tiṣya days [i.e., when the moon is in the constellation containing Tiṣya, Sirius]; it may also be proclaimed in the intervals between those days; and on appropriate occasions it may be read to individuals.

By doing this, you will be carrying out my commands.

The Edicts of Aśoka

B. Particular Applications

I. RESTRICTIONS ON FEASTS AND THE SLAUGHTERING OF ANIMALS; PARDONING PRISONERS

Rock Edict I

King Priyadarśī has commanded this edict on Dharma to be inscribed:

No living creature shall be slaughtered here [at Pāṭaliputra, Aśoka's capital city], and no festive gatherings shall be held. King Priyadarśī sees a great many evils in festive gatherings. Yet he also approves of some kinds of festivals.

Many hundreds of thousand living creatures were formerly slaughtered every day for curries in the kitchens of His Majesty. At present, when this edict on Dharma is inscribed, only three living creatures are killed daily, two peacocks and a deer, and the deer is not slaughtered regularly. In the future, not even these three animals shall be slaughtered.

Pillar Edict V

King Priyadarśī says:

Twenty-six years after my coronation I declared that the following animals were not to be killed: parrots, mynas, the *aruṇa*, ruddy geese, wild geese, the *nandīmukha*, pigeons [or cranes], bats, queen ants, terrapins, boneless fish [probably prawns], the *vedaveyaka*, the *pupuṭa* of the Ganges, skates, tortoises and porcupines, squirrels, twelve-antler stags, bulls which have been set free, household animals and vermin, rhinoceroses, white pigeons, domestic pigeons, and all quadrupeds which are not useful or edible.[10]

She-goats, ewes, and sows which have young or are in milk, and also their young less than six months old, must not be killed.

Cocks must not be made into capons.

Husks which contain living creatures must not be burned.

Forests must not be burned without reason or in order to kill living creatures.

Living animals must not be fed to other animals.

Fish must not be killed or sold on the day of the full moon which begins each of the three seasons, on the Tiṣya [Sirius] full moon, on the three days which end a fortnight and begin a new one, or on fast days [a total of fifty-six days during each year].

On those same days, animals which live in the elephant forests and the fishermen's preserves must not be killed.

On the eighth day of the fortnight, on the fourteenth and fifteenth, on Tiṣya and Punarvasu [probably one of the Pleiades] days, on the full moon day beginning each season, and on festival days, bulls, he-

[10] The names of the animals left in Prākrit are unknown or doubtful.

goats, rams, boars, and other animals which are usually castrated must not be castrated.

On Tiṣya and Punarvasu days and during the fortnight of each seasonal full moon, horses and bullocks must not be branded.

During the twenty-six years since my coronation, I have ordered the release of prisoners twenty-five times.

2. PUBLIC ADMINISTRATION: THE PROMULGATION OF MORALITY AND THE ADMINISTRATION OF JUSTICE

Rock Edict III

King Priyadarśī says:

Twelve years after my coronation I ordered the following:

Everywhere in my dominions local, provincial, and state officials shall make a tour of their districts every five years to proclaim the following precepts of Dharma as well as to transact other business:

Obedience to mother and father; liberality to friends, acquaintances, relatives, priests, and ascetics; abstention from killing living creatures; and moderation in spending money and acquiring possessions are all meritorious.

The Council shall direct local officials concerning the execution of these orders in accordance with my instruction and my intention.

Rock Edict V [continued from IV. 2]

In the past there were no officers charged with spreading Dharma. I created these posts in the thirteenth year of my reign.

These officers are commissioned to work with all sects in establishing and promoting Dharma, in seeing to the welfare and happiness of all those devoted to

Dharma, among the Yōnas, Kambōjas, Gandhāras, Rāṣṭrikas, Pitinikas, and other peoples living on the western borders of my kingdom. They are commissioned to work among the soldiers and their chiefs, the ascetics and householders, the poor and the aged, to secure the welfare and happiness and release from imprisonment of those devoted to Dharma. They are also commissioned to work among prisoners to distribute money to those who have many children, to secure the release of those who were instigated to crime by others, and to pardon those who are very aged.

They have been assigned everywhere—here [at Pāṭaliputra], in all the provincial towns, and in the harems of my brothers and sisters and other relatives. These officers in charge of spreading Dharma are at work everywhere in my dominions among people devoted to Dharma, whether they are only inclined to Dharma or established in Dharma or duly devoted to charity.

I have commanded this edict on Dharma to be inscribed so that it may last forever and so that my descendants may conform to it.

Pillar Edict IV

King Priyadarśi says:

I ordered this edict on Dharma inscribed twenty-six years after my coronation.

I have appointed provincial governors [Rājūkas]

to serve as administrators over hundreds of thousands of people.

In order that they may be fearless and impartial in administering the welfare and happiness of the people of the provinces and in bestowing favors among them, I have left to the discretion of these governors the award of honors and the infliction of punishments.

They shall learn the sources of the people's happiness and misery, and they shall admonish the people of the provinces, with the help of those who are devoted to Dharma, to lead lives that will gain them happiness in this world and the next.

The provincial governors are, of course, ready to obey me. They shall also obey the officers of higher rank [Puruṣas], who are acquainted with my wishes and who will also instruct the people, in order that the provincial governors will be able to please and serve me.

Just as a man feels confident when he has intrusted his child to a skilled nurse, thinking, "This skilled nurse will take good care of my child," so I have appointed the provincial governors for the welfare and happiness of my provincial people.

In order that they may perform their duties fearlessly, confidently, and cheerfully, they have been given discretion in the distribution of honors and the infliction of punishments.

Impartiality is desirable in legal procedures and in

punishments. I have therefore decreed that henceforth prisoners who have been convicted and sentenced to death shall be granted a respite of three days. [During this period their] relatives may appeal to the officials for the prisoners' lives; or, if no one makes an appeal, the prisoners may prepare for the other world by distributing gifts or by fasting.

For I desire that, when the period of respite has expired, they may attain happiness in the next world, and that various ways of practicing Dharma by self-control and the distribution of gifts may be increased among the people.

Kaliṅga Edict I

King Priyadarśī orders the following instructions to be transmitted to his officials at Tosalī:[11]

Whenever something right comes to my attention, I want it put into practice and I want effective means devised to achieve it. My principal means to do this is to transmit my instructions to you. For I have placed you in charge of thousands of people to obtain their affection for me.

All men are my children. Just as I seek the welfare

[11] The Dhauli texts reads Samāpā. The two Kaliṅga Rock Edicts are found only at Dhauli and Jaugaḍa. Kaliṅga Edicts I and II begin in the same fashion; but after proclaiming that all men are his children, Aśoka proceeds in Kaliṅga Edict II to instructions concerning relations to neighboring states (see above, VI. A. 4), while in Kaliṅga Edict I he turns his attention to instructions concerning the administration of justice.

and happiness of my own children in this world and the next, I seek the same things for all men. You do not understand this desire of mine fully. Some of you may understand it, but even those grasp it only partially, not fully. However elevated your position, you must give it your attention.

Sometimes in the administration of justice a person will suffer imprisonment or torture. When this happens, he sometimes dies accidentally, and many other people suffer because of this.

In such circumstances, you must try to follow the middle path [that is, justice or moderation]. Envy, anger, cruelty, impatience, lack of application, laziness, and fatigue interfere with the attainment of this middle path. Therefore, each of you should try to be sure that you are not possessed by these passions.

The key to success in this endeavor is not to become angry and not to hurry. The tired administrator will not advance, but you should move, advance, and progress. Your supervisors must tell you, "Put all your effort to carrying out the duties assigned to you by the King. Such and such are the instructions of the Beloved of the Gods."

The observance of this injunction will produce great good; failure to observe it will produce great harm. For if you fail to observe it, you will attain neither heaven nor the King's favor. The reason for this extreme thought is that a double gain is procured by observing this duty, for by carrying it out properly you will gain heaven and also satisfy your obligations to me.

This edict must be read to all on every Tiṣya day. It may be read even to individuals on suitable occasions at other times. If you do this you will be able to carry out your duty.

This edict has been inscribed here to remind the judicial officers in this city to try at all times to avoid unjust imprisonment or unjust torture. To the same end I shall send out every five years an official who will not be harsh or cruel but gentle, and his assignment will be to see that the judicial officers are following my instructions. Moreover, the prince who governs the city of Ujjayinī will send out the same kind of officials at least every three years. An official will be sent out from Takṣaśilā also. These officials will not neglect their own duties, but they will also check to see whether the local judicial officers are carrying out the King's instructions.

Rock Edict II

Everywhere in the dominions of King Priyadarśī, as well as in the border territories of the Choḷas, the Pāṇḍyas, the Satiyaputra, the Keralaputra [all in the southern tip of the Indian peninsula], the Ceylonese, the Yōna king named Antiochos, and those kings who are neighbors of Antiochos—everywhere provision has been made for two kinds of medical treatment, treatment for men and for animals.

Medicinal herbs, suitable for men and animals, have been imported and planted wherever they were not previously available. Also, where roots and fruits were lacking, they have been imported and planted.

Wells have been dug and trees planted along the roads for the use of men and animals.

Pillar Edict VII [continued from IV. 1]

King Priyadarśī says:

I have ordered banyan trees to be planted along the roads to give shade to men and animals. I have ordered mango groves to be planted. I have ordered wells to be dug every half-kos [about a half-mile], and I have ordered rest houses built. I have had many watering stations built for the convenience of men and animals.

These are trifling comforts. For the people have received various facilities from previous kings as well as from me. But I have done what I have primarily in order that the people may follow the path of Dharma with faith and devotion.

4. BUDDHISM AND THE ĀJĪVIKA SECT

Maskī Rock Edict

Aśoka, Beloved of the Gods,[12] issues the following proclamation:

For more than two and a half years, I have been a lay disciple [upāsaka] of the Buddha. More than a year ago, I visited the Saṁgha [the Buddhist religious orders], and since then I have been energetic in my efforts.

[The edict continues by proclaiming the way to the gods open to poor and rich alike by the practice of Dharma; see above, VI. A. 2.]

Bhabra Rock Edict

King Priyadarśī of Magadha conveys his greetings to the Saṁgha and wishes them good health and prosperity.

You know, Reverend Sirs, the extent of my reverence for and faith in the Buddha, the Dharma, and the Saṁgha.

Whatever the Lord Buddha has said, Reverend Sirs, is of course well said. But it is proper for me to enumerate the texts which express true Dharma and which may make it everlasting.

The following, Reverend Sirs, are the texts on Dharma:

[12] The King's name, Aśoka, is used in the Maskī text; King Aśoka, Aśokarāja, in the Gujarra text.

The Exaltation of Moral Discipline [*Vinaya-samu-kasa*]

The Modes of Ideal Life [*aliya-vasāṇi*]

Fears of the Future [*Anāgata-bhayāni*]

The Song of the Hermits [*Muni-gāthā*]

Discourse on the Saintly Life [*Mauneya-sūte*]

The Questions of Upatiṣya [*Upatisa-pasine*], and also

The Sermon to Rāhula [*Rāhulavāda*], which was delivered by the Lord Buddha on the subject of falsehood.

It is my desire, Reverend Sirs, that many monks and nuns listen to these texts on Dharma frequently and meditate on them. The lay disciples, both men and women, should do the same.

I have ordered this edict to be inscribed, Reverend Sirs, in order that they may know my intention.

Sāñchī Pillar Edict

[The opening lines of the edict, which were probably addressed to Aśoka's officials at Sāñchī, are mutilated. The expression "be divided" is legible in this portion, and the instructions are clearly for measures to prevent the disruption of the Saṁgha.]

The Saṁgha of the monks and the Saṁgha of the nuns have each been united to continue united as long as my sons and great-grandsons rule and as long as the sun and moon shine.

The monk or nun who disrupts the Saṁgha shall

be required to put on white robes [instead of the customary yellow] and to live in non-residence (*anabasasi*). It is my desire that the Saṁgha be united and endure forever.

Sarnath Pillar Edict

[The opening three lines of the edict are mutilated. The fragmentary remains suggest that King Priyadarśī instructs his officials, probably those stationed at Pāṭaliputra, to take precautions that] no one shall disrupt the Saṁgha.

If a monk or nun disrupts the Saṁgha, he or she shall be required to put on a white robe and to live in non-residence.

This edict should be published both in the Saṁgha of the monks and in the Saṁgha of the nuns.

King Priyadarśī says:

Place one copy of this edict in the cloister of the vihāra; give another copy to the lay disciples. The lay disciples shall assemble every fast day to study this edict. Every official shall regularly attend services on every fast day in order to familiarize himself with the edict and understand it fully.

Moreover you [i.e., Aśoka's officials at Pāṭaliputra] shall send orders throughout the district under your administration putting this edict into effect. Your subordinates shall do the same in all fortified towns and the districts surrounding them.

The Edicts of Aśoka

Twenty years after his coronation, King Priyadarśī, Beloved of the Gods, visited this place in person
and worshiped here because the Buddha, the Sage
of the Śākyas, was born here.

He ordered a stone wall to be constructed around
the place and erected this stone pillar to commemorate his visit.

He declared the village of Lummini [now Rum-
mindei] free of taxes and required to pay only one-
eighth of its produce [about half the usual amount]
as land revenue.

Karna Chaupar Cave Edict[13]

King Priyadarśī, nineteen years after his coronation, dedicated this cave, in the very pleasant Khalatika Hill, beyond the floods of the rainy season.

[13] In the Barābar Hills seven caves have been found, usually
referred to as the Barābar (four) and the Nāgārjuni (three).
Three of the Barābar caves contain Aśokan inscriptions. Five of the
seven caves were dedicated for the use of ascetics of the Ājīvika
sect. Barābar Hill was called Khalatika Hill in Aśoka's time.